# God is good, y'all!

## INSPIRATIONS TO BLESS YOUR HEART

## KEN PETERSEN

*General Editor*

Tyndale House Publishers, Inc.
CAROL STREAM, ILLINOIS

**LIVING EXPRESSIONS** COLLECTION

*Living Expressions* invites you to explore God's Word and express your creativity in ways that are refreshing to the spirit and restorative to the soul.

Visit Tyndale online at www.tyndale.com.

*TYNDALE*, Tyndale's quill logo, *Living Expressions*, and the Living Expressions logo are registered trademarks of Tyndale House Publishers, Inc.

*God Is Good, Y'all! Inspirations to Bless Your Heart*

Designed by Ron C. Kaufmann

For information about special discounts for bulk purchases, please contact Tyndale House Publishers at csresponse@tyndale.com, or call 1-800-323-9400.

ISBN 978-1-4964-3961-1

Printed in China

25   24   23   22   21   20   19
7    6    5    4    3    2    1

# Contents

I am confident

I will see the LORD's goodness

while I am here in the land of the living.

PSALM 27:13

God
is good,
y'all!

# How great is our God!

We often say "God is good" when positive things happen to us, but it's important to remember that his goodness goes way beyond the happy things he throws our way. God not only *does* good things; he *is* good! God's goodness means he is the very embodiment of truth, love, justice, and righteousness. Out of his virtuous character, God provided his own Son, Jesus, as a sacrifice on the cross for our redemption—our eternal salvation. Remember this when someday you are faced with a health scare, a difficult situation, or even the death of someone close to you. Amid the bad things that happen, God demonstrates his boundless love, comfort, and compassion. With his help, we will still be able to say, "God is good, y'all!"

Taste and see that the LORD is good. Oh, the joys of those who take refuge in him!

**PSALM 34:8**

Great is the LORD! He is most worthy of praise! No one can measure his greatness.

**PSALM 145:3**

# Cherishing the ones who matter most

You well know that biscuits and gravy made from scratch is a special kind of goodness—not only because of its mouth-watering taste but also because it reminds you of home sweet home: the familiar comforts and pleasures . . . the happy memories made with those you love. No one's more important than family. Yet maybe you haven't shown how much you cherish yours lately. Perhaps now is a good time to remember the specific things that make your family members so special. Praise God for putting each one in your life. Then maybe at some blessed time today, whisper to them, "I love you like biscuits and gravy!"

Whatever is true, whatever is noble, whatever is right, whatever is pure, whatever is lovely, whatever is admirable—if anything is excellent or praiseworthy—think about such things.

PHILIPPIANS 4:8, NIV

Most important of all, continue to show deep love for each other, for love covers a multitude of sins.

1 PETER 4:8

I love you
like biscuits
and gravy

You'd best get glad in the same britches you got mad in

# When you get too full of yourself

Have you ever gotten all steamed up because you were sure you were right about something, but others disagreed? You were madder than a wet hen, and it spiraled into a bigger and bigger problem. Sometimes, though, the real problem *is* us. We can be so loud and pushy when we demand we're right that we end up making our own enemies and messes. There are words for this—*pride* and *self-righteousness*—and the Bible advises that we'd best get busy being glad in the same britches we got mad in. In other words, we need to get over ourselves, deal with the matter, let go of our pride, and start to value others more highly. Do you need to confess to God that you've gotten too big for your britches? Turn the situation over to him and see what he will do—not only in the mess you find yourself in, but also in your heart and character.

> Do nothing out of selfish ambition or vain conceit. Rather, in humility value others above yourselves.
>
> **PHILIPPIANS 2:3, NIV**

# Abiding in the hope of heaven

Have you heard the gospel tune "Will You Meet Me Over Yonder?" It's about Christian families and friends being reunited in heaven. The beautiful thing about the Christian life is its ultimate promise: eternal life. Here on earth, we enjoy fellowship with God through his Holy Spirit, and when we pass away, we'll be welcomed into his heavenly home. Maybe for you it feels too soon to think about such matters. But when you have heaven on your mind, your life on earth could never be better. So don't be afraid to give some thought to the joys of life over yonder. See how it changes your outlook today.

Now we live with great expectation, and we have a priceless inheritance—an inheritance that is kept in heaven for you, pure and undefiled, beyond the reach of change and decay.

1 PETER 1:3-4

Since you have been raised to new life with Christ, set your sights on the realities of heaven, where Christ sits in the place of honor.

COLOSSIANS 3:1

Over
yonder

# When your tongue gets the best of you

You know someone this applies to, don't you? Someone who chatters and gossips and often says things that hurt others. Even if you haven't said it to their face, you've probably thought it. But if you turn the mirror around, can you see yourself? If you're honest, can you remember a time you said too much about someone? As one who loves Jesus, you have a higher calling. He wants you to carry yourself with dignity and respect as he would instead of hogging the conversation and speaking ill of people. Pray for him to help you tell the Good News *to* others and not repeat the gossipy news *about* others.

Though some tongues just love the taste of gossip, those who follow Jesus have better uses for language than that. Don't talk dirty or silly. That kind of talk doesn't fit our style. Thanksgiving is our dialect.

**EPHESIANS 5:4, MSG**

# When doing nothing is the best thing

The Bible says there is "a time for every activity under heaven" (Ecclesiastes 3:1). Sure, there's a time for you to get up off the couch and do something. But maybe, just maybe, it's time for you to pause and wait—to sit down and put your feet up. Lollygaggin' isn't always a bad thing. The Bible also says we are to wait upon the Lord. Sometimes it's important to stop all our busyness and focus on God so we can rest up, both spiritually and physically. You might want to do some lollygaggin' by reading the Scriptures, listening for the Lord's voice, and preparing yourself for the great things he will do. And don't worry or feel guilty, 'cause this kind of lollygaggin' is never a waste of time!

They that wait upon the LORD shall renew their strength; they shall mount up with wings as eagles; they shall run, and not be weary; and they shall walk, and not faint.

**ISAIAH 40:31, KJV**

I'm
just
lolly-
gaggin'

That dog
won't hunt

# Finding help when life doesn't work

Maybe you're experiencing a spell when everything seems impossible. That dog just won't hunt. When you try and try and nothing succeeds, it's easy to spiral downward into hopelessness. But like Hazel says in Fannie Flagg's novel *I Still Dream about You*, "Don't give up before the miracle happens." When you're failing and flailing, come to God in your despair. See if he will change the circumstances and outcomes—or at least the way you handle them. Listen to him perhaps telling you to try something different. Let him speak new hope and possibility over you. He wants you to succeed. But even more, he wants you to seek him and spend time in his presence.

I will never forget this awful time, as I grieve over my loss. Yet I still dare to hope when I remember this: The faithful love of the LORD never ends! His mercies never cease. Great is his faithfulness.

LAMENTATIONS 3:20-23

Jesus looked at them and said, "With man this is impossible, but with God all things are possible."

MATTHEW 19:26, ESV

# Focusing on what's most important

Take a moment to reflect on those things in life that matter most. Is your to-do list focused on them, or are you fussing about a hundred little things instead? When Jesus was visiting with Mary and Martha, he observed how Martha was fit to be tied when she was trying to cook up supper while Mary sat at his feet focusing on what was most important in her life. Sure, there's always a heap of stuff that's waiting to be whupped—but don't get distracted by it. You've got bigger fish to fry. Sit at Jesus' feet, quiet your heart, and listen to what he says. Time spent with the Lord is never wasted.

The Lord said to her, "My dear Martha, you are worried and upset over all these details! There is only one thing worth being concerned about. Mary has discovered it, and it will not be taken away from her."

LUKE 10:41-42

Be still, and know that I am God! I will be honored by every nation. I will be honored throughout the world.

PSALM 46:10

# Overcoming perfectionism

Maybe you grew up in a home where minding manners was of the utmost importance. And maybe today you're a perfectionist. If you find yourself always needing to appear at your best in front of others, that's a problem; and it's holding you back from meaningful, honest relationships. It's okay to drop the act. Stop pretending. Ask God to help you be yourself, imperfections and all. Understand that he defines perfection not in behavioral terms but as a commitment to persevere in faith. In time, his power will transform and perfect all his kids. So relax! An honest and authentic walk with Jesus is the perfection God wants.

I don't mean to say that I have already achieved these things or that I have already reached perfection. But I press on to possess that perfection for which Christ Jesus first possessed me. No, dear brothers and sisters, I have not achieved it, but I focus on this one thing: Forgetting the past and looking forward to what lies ahead, I press on to reach the end of the race and receive the heavenly prize.

PHILIPPIANS 3:12-14

# Sharing the Good News

Jesus came to save sinners, heal the sick, and proclaim God's Kingdom. When he invited Peter and Andrew to leave their fishing careers and follow him, he promised them a better gig: fishing for people! The heart of Jesus is to bring the Good News of salvation and new life to the world. When he touches us with his love, it's hard to keep his goodness a secret. Not everyone is called to be an evangelist, but never underestimate the impact your story could have on others. Whether you simply bless them with encouragement or lead them to life-changing personal faith, it's always a good day when you can do a little fishin'.

As Jesus was walking along the shore of the Sea of Galilee, he saw two brothers—Simon, also called Peter, and Andrew—throwing a net into the water, for they fished for a living. Jesus called out to them, "Come, follow me, and I will show you how to fish for people!" And they left their nets at once and followed him.

MATTHEW 4:18-20

Fish
or cut
bait

Life
needs more
sweet tea
and
sunshine

# Brightening the world around you

Has the world around you become dark? Does life right now taste about as sour as a bucket of fresh lemons? Sometimes it just turns out that way. Here's a suggestion: Don't get overwhelmed. Just find one thing you can do or one person whose life you can brighten and add some sugar to. When we focus on blessing others, our own problems often seem less burdensome. Proverbs 11:25 reminds us that "the generous will prosper; those who refresh others will themselves be refreshed." How can *you* be sweet tea and sunshine today?

Dear friends, I am not writing a new commandment for you; rather it is an old one you have had from the very beginning. This old commandment—to love one another—is the same message you heard before. Yet it is also new. Jesus lived the truth of this commandment, and you also are living it. For the darkness is disappearing, and the true light is already shining.

1 JOHN 2:7-8

# Finding strength in weakness

The Bible is filled with interesting characters: kings and prophets, outcasts and beggars, heroes and villains. Some are remembered for their acts of courage, while others are noteworthy for their tenacity and fortitude. When God's messenger declared that Sarah would soon have a baby, she laughed. Not surprising, *considering she was ninety*. But God was faithful. Within a year, she was cradling Isaac in her arms. Sarah had endured infertility, odd looks, and childbirth at an age when many of her old-lady friends already had great-grandchildren. Talk about tough! As God's girl, you're in good company with Sarah—tough as a pine knot. Ask for his wisdom and strength to tackle every obstacle with confidence, knowing he will transform your weakness into his strength.

[Jesus] said, "My grace is all you need. My power works best in weakness." . . . That's why I take pleasure in my weaknesses, and in the insults . . . that I suffer for Christ. For when I am weak, then I am strong.

2 CORINTHIANS 12:9-10

# It'll knock you into the middle of next week

# Turning to Jesus in hard times

Has something hit you hard just now? A financial setback?
A job change? Maybe a medical scare or the death of someone
close to you? What is it this week that has knocked you back
on your heels? Jesus says, "Here on earth you will have many
trials and sorrows. But take heart, because I have overcome the
world" (John 16:33). The world may have thrown you a sucker
punch, but Jesus has your back. Because he has overcome, so
will you. Meanwhile, the yuck in life can teach us about God's
faithfulness and reveal his purposes more clearly. In fact, God
might be using the hardships you're going through these days
to prepare you for something big. Be still right now and let the
truth of God's Word encourage you.

Be truly glad. There is wonderful joy ahead, even
though you must endure many trials for a little while.
These trials will show that your faith is genuine. It
is being tested as fire tests and purifies gold.

**1 PETER 1:6-7**

# Proof there is hope for your loved ones

If you think your family is dysfunctional, take a look in the first chapter of the Gospel of Matthew at the lineage for one of the most messed-up families ever. Pastors often skip over reading this passage in church to avoid boring their audience; yet it communicates a very important message. Within that long list are some people who made serious mistakes in life, but at the very end comes Jesus—God incarnate, the Savior of the world. You see, God uses our own failures *as well as* the shortcomings of our parents and children to accomplish his great purposes. The Bible says that God can redeem any person, any family, any heritage to reflect his image. Today, take courage and comfort knowing that not even your own crazy family is beyond the reach of God's grace.

Believe in the Lord Jesus and you will be saved,
along with everyone in your household.

ACTS 16:31

Adam's one sin brings condemnation for everyone,
but Christ's one act of righteousness brings a right
relationship with God and new life for everyone.

ROMANS 5:18

If you met
my family,
you'd
understand

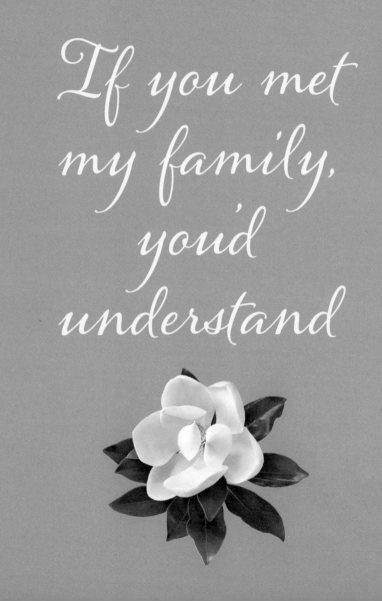

Pretty as a peach

# Preparing for fruitfulness

We think of peaches as warm-weather fruit. They are, but did you know peach trees require the chillier temperatures that winter brings? Only by resting in the cold do they produce beautiful, sweet fruit. The same is true of us spiritually. Maybe this is a bleak season for you, and you're discouraged in your faith. Remember, it's important to step back and see God's larger picture—the full cycle of seasons and growth he has planned for you. It may be nippy right now, but that's preparation for the abundant harvest ahead. Spend time resting with God, and wait with anticipation for the luscious fruit he'll grow in your life. It's gonna be worth it!

We ask God to give you complete knowledge of his will and to give you spiritual wisdom and understanding. Then the way you live will always honor and please the Lord, and your lives will produce every kind of good fruit. All the while, you will grow as you learn to know God better and better.

COLOSSIANS 1:9-10

# Understanding the power of words

Words—the Bible talks a lot about them. God used words to create the world: "God said, 'Let there be light,' and there was light" (Genesis 1:3). Jesus is called *the Word*: "The Word was with God, and the Word was God" (John 1:1). Wise Solomon warns, "The tongue can bring death or life" (Proverbs 18:21). Are you noticing a pattern? Words have power! By speaking words that emphasize the positive aspects of a person or situation, we create an atmosphere of life and hope. When we utter words charged with negativity or hate, we add a palpable layer of gloom and despair to our surroundings. So what've you got to lose? Go ahead and clear the air. Make a habit of declaring those things "that are excellent and worthy of praise" (Philippians 4:8), and become a cocreator with Jesus in establishing his Kingdom reign here on earth.

If you want to enjoy life and see many happy days, keep your tongue from speaking evil and your lips from telling lies.

**1 PETER 3:10**

Well,
I
declare!

# When you get hot under the collar

It seems there's a person in everyone's life who's just plain bothersome. With them, there's always a conflict, always a problem . . . just always *something*. Who in your life is like that—the one who manages to ruffle your feathers? You know, the Bible has a solution for handling that kind of mess, but it's advice you wouldn't expect. It says that love believes the best about others. And when you look for the best in those around you, it changes your attitude toward them—and that may change their behavior toward you. Jesus is saying, "Just as I have loved you, you should love each other" (John 13:34). See what happens when you obey Jesus and approach this other person in love.

> Love . . . doesn't fly off the handle, doesn't keep score of the sins of others. . . . [Love] always looks for the best, never looks back, but keeps going to the end.
>
> 1 CORINTHIANS 13:5-7, MSG

# Praying with perseverance

Jesus told a story about a widow who'd gotten the raw end of a deal. She took the matter to a judge, but he could have cared less about her plight. Yet the lady wouldn't give up! She kept bugging him until he finally granted her justice—just to get her off his back. "The Lord said, 'Learn a lesson from this unjust judge. Even he rendered a just decision in the end. So don't you think God will surely give justice to his chosen people who cry out to him day and night?'" (Luke 18:6-7). Don't give up on asking God to fulfill his promises in your life. Be the squeaky wheel! Have patience and know that he hears your prayers. In due time, the Lord will honor your persistence and grant your request. Then let the oil of his joy quiet your heart with peace and thanksgiving.

You love justice and hate evil. Therefore God, your God, has anointed you, pouring out the oil of joy.

**PSALM 45:7**

Always pray and never give up.

**LUKE 18:1**

The squeaky wheel gets the grease

Plumb
tuckered
out

# When life leaves you tired yet unable to sleep

Have life's challenges left you exhausted? It's strange, but at times we're so drained that we actually struggle to fall asleep. Whether or not there's a medical explanation for this oxymoron, the result is that we're caught in a vicious cycle of fatigue and despair. The next time you're restless at night, take a deep breath. Lay down your troubles before Jesus, and let him shoulder your burdens. Imagine yourself relaxing in his arms. Try singing a favorite hymn while you meditate on its words. Perhaps listening to worship music or an audio version of the Bible will help calm your heart. Above all, cling to the promise that "God gives rest to his loved ones" (Psalm 127:2).

Let me remember my song in the night;
let me meditate in my heart.

PSALM 77:6, ESV

Jesus said, "Come to me, all of you who are weary and carry heavy burdens, and I will give you rest. . . . I am humble and gentle at heart, and you will find rest for your souls."

MATTHEW 11:28-29

# The enduring value of friendship

If you have a bestie—a BFF—a soul sister you can count on, you know it's a blessing to be two peas in a pod, sharing similar interests and helping each other through life. Trustworthy friends are hard to come by! The Bible says that when David and Jonathan met, they "had an immediate bond." Only God could deliver such a divine gift. Whether or not you've experienced that kind of friendship, there's someone who longs to be your closest companion. Jesus laid down his life for us all, and he's reaching out to you now. Will you take his hand?

After David had finished talking with Saul, he met Jonathan, the king's son. There was an immediate bond between them, for Jonathan loved David. . . . And Jonathan made a solemn pact with David, because he loved him as he loved himself.

**1 SAMUEL 18:1-3**

[Jesus said,] "Love each other in the same way I have loved you. There is no greater love than to lay down one's life for one's friends."

**JOHN 15:12-13**

Two peas
in a pod

Hold your
horses—
he ain't
done yet

# When you feel like a failure

Something bad has happened—at home, or at school, or at work—and it points back at you. Suddenly you're feeling like you've come up short—as in, you've failed. It's making you question everything and doubt yourself. Well, just wait a minute. Don't know if you've heard this yet, but no one is perfect. Everyone fails; it's part of life and learning. Remember that God is still at work behind the scenes . . . teaching you, shaping you, helping you grow. In the Creator's hands, you're one beautiful work in progress. So hold your horses—he ain't done yet.

"I know the plans I have for you," declares the LORD, "plans to prosper you and not to harm you, plans to give you hope and a future."

JEREMIAH 29:11, NIV

God is working in you, giving you the desire and the power to do what pleases him.

PHILIPPIANS 2:13

# Discovering the God of surprises

Has life become humdrum and routine? Think about how Jesus often surprised those around him. One woman was simply pursuing her humdrum task of fetching water at the well when she came upon Jesus sitting there. He asked her for a drink. *Oh my stars!* she probably thought. The woman was surprised that he would even talk with her since she was a Samaritan and he was a Jew. "She said to Jesus, '. . . Why are you asking me for a drink?'" (John 4:9). Yet Jesus continued their conversation, and at every turn, Jesus surprised her. He knew everything about her and turned her life around for the better. In the routine of your day and week, why not sit a spell with Jesus? Let him surprise you with what he has in store.

> The woman left her water jar beside the well and ran back to the village, telling everyone, "Come and see a man who told me everything I ever did! Could he possibly be the Messiah?"
>
> JOHN 4:28-29

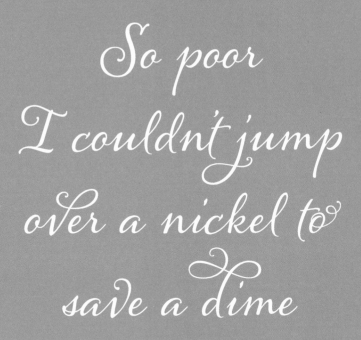

So poor
I couldn't jump
over a nickel to
save a dime

# Trusting God for true wealth

Money gotcha down? Whether you have no income, live paycheck to paycheck, or just wish you had a little extra fat in your wallet, you're not alone. But God created us to experience the abundance that flows from his character. Of course, we know full well his abundance isn't confined to material blessings since true wealth is not defined by the sum of our worldly assets. But when you're struggling to put food on the table or pay the rent or your family's medical bills . . . well, *tough* doesn't begin to describe it. Whatever your situation, commit today to depend on God as your source. He will make a way. Whether he drops money in your lap, blesses you with a new job, or simply fills you with peace that he'll make a way . . . you can't lose. With him, there is no lack.

Beloved, I pray that in every way you may prosper and enjoy good health, as your soul also prospers.

3 JOHN 1:2, BSB

True godliness with contentment is itself great wealth.

1 TIMOTHY 6:6

# Savoring the life God has given you

Think about all the Lord has given you—not just your "stuff" but also family, friends, relationships. Is it hard to imagine being without these special treasures in your life? Now savor this: The God of the universe personally cares about you, and if you have come to Jesus for the forgiveness and new life that he offers, then he talks with you and walks with you! His words, the Bible says, "are sweeter than honey" (Psalm 119:103). He takes great delight in you—in fact, "the LORD, whose very name is Jealous, is a God who is jealous about his relationship with you" (Exodus 34:14). So keep relishing your life with God, and enjoy all he has provided.

Teach those who are rich in this world not to be proud and not to trust in their money, which is so unreliable. Their trust should be in God, who richly gives us all we need for our enjoyment.

1 TIMOTHY 6:17

Those who rely on faith are blessed.

GALATIANS 3:9, NIV

Sweeter than sweet potato pie

Is it a doohickey,
a whatchamacallit,
or a thingamajig?

# When life leaves you discombobulated

Have you ever forgotten what something is called? Misplaced something you'd seen only moments ago? Of course! We all have. It's likely that in the past year, you've walked into a room to fetch something, only to scratch your head trying to remember what it was. Whether you're experiencing muddled thoughts or a more serious memory condition, God's whisper can be heard though the noise. When your mind becomes overwhelmed by life, take a break—sit down, go for a walk, or simply close your eyes and focus. In these moments, ask God to deliver you from the chaos. Let his voice be the only thing you hear. As he speaks directly into your thoughts, allow his words to calm your troubled mind and reassure your heart.

God has not given us a spirit of fear, but of
power and of love and of a sound mind.

2 TIMOTHY 1:7, NKJV

Prepare your minds for action and exercise self-control.
Put all your hope in the gracious salvation that will come
to you when Jesus Christ is revealed to the world.

1 PETER 1:13

# Seeing yourself as God sees you

Maybe the family's been raving about your new recipe for fried chicken and collard greens, or perhaps you recently wowed coworkers with a stellar presentation at the office. You'd suppose that would be enough to boost your spirits, right? But you still get down on yourself. *It just wasn't all that great*, you think. Often we burden ourselves with messages of how we fall short. We're afraid to accept our true value. Jesus gives us a peek at his perspective on those who follow him: "You are the light of the world. . . . No one lights a lamp and then puts it under a basket" (Matthew 5:14-15). You are one of his chosen, destined to transform the world around you. He sees the good you do, and he approves. Don't doubt what God affirms. God is for you. He thinks it tastes pretty good *because* you made it.

> We are his workmanship, created in Christ Jesus for good works, which God prepared beforehand, that we should walk in them.
>
> EPHESIANS 2:10, ESV

Tastes

pretty good—

even if I

did make it

Gimme

some

sugar

# When life turns sour

Sometimes a day or even a whole week turns bad. Stuff happens that is unexpected, disappointing, frustrating. Every simple action feels overwhelming. Are you tasting nothing but vinegar this week? Are you longing for some sugar in your life—just a little something to sweeten the sour? Remember, you're not alone. The psalmist writes, "I'm caught in a maze and can't find my way out, blinded by tears of pain and frustration" (Psalm 88:8-9, MSG). The Bible encourages us to take our bitter moments to God in prayer. The sugar he gives is his kiss of peace, which seals in us the assurance of his care.

Don't worry about anything; instead, pray about everything. Tell God what you need, and thank him for all he has done. Then you will experience God's peace, which exceeds anything we can understand. His peace will guard your hearts and minds as you live in Christ Jesus.

**PHILIPPIANS 4:6-7**

# Seeking the will of God each day

Our lives are so busy! To keep up with full agendas, we end up racing through our chores, duties, and lists. Unfortunately, this often means we rush through life without really seeking what God wants. But what if we were to walk through our days asking God what his will is for us in each moment? Is that even possible? Well, it doesn't take much to say this simple prayer: "What would you have me do, Lord?" Why not try that today? Then listen and let God give you his answer. Through this simple act of submission, he'll work through your life in amazing ways. And each day, you'll come to know him even better.

May your Kingdom come soon. May your will
be done on earth, as it is in heaven.

MATTHEW 6:10

Be careful how you live. Don't live like fools, but
like those who are wise. Make the most of every
opportunity in these evil days. Don't act thoughtlessly,
but understand what the Lord wants you to do.

EPHESIANS 5:15-17

Can't
never
could

# When you're discouraged and can't move a step

Whoever came up with the phrase "Can't never could" was pretty smart. And you know the truth of it—that you'll never conquer life's challenges if you don't try. Still, when you feel stuck, it's as if someone has died but there's no funeral. Basically, you're deep in the nothing of life and can't take a step. But never underestimate the power of the almighty, omnipotent Creator of the universe—who cares about you so much that he's numbered the hairs on your head. God can put you on your feet again. So what are you waiting for? Ask him to lift you out of the pit, and open yourself to his strength and joy and love. He wants you to walk forward again with confidence and hope. Can't never could, but with God on your side, you "*can* do everything through Christ" (Philippians 4:13, emphasis added).

The very hairs on your head are all numbered. So don't be afraid; you are more valuable to God than a whole flock of sparrows.

LUKE 12:7

# Practicing the art of patience

Some would rank hot corn bread among the best vittles on the planet. Still, you can't take the pan out of the oven too soon, or someone will sink their teeth into a mess of gooey batter in the middle. That delicious supper you're planning demands patience! Sometimes when we're excited about the dreams we have for our lives—a special relationship, a promotion, a move to a new place—we grow impatient waiting for them to happen. We're ready, and we're tired of waiting. But the Bible reminds us how important it is to let things happen in God's timing. Maybe the corn bread is still wet. Our heavenly Father knows what's best for us, what needs to "cook" more, and what the final outcome will be. He wants us to pause in our busy lives and give him our full attention. So take a breath. Control that urge to open the oven door. Give the Lord your focus and love, and see what his perfect timing is all about.

Be still in the presence of the LORD, and
wait patiently for him to act.

**PSALM 37:7**

His corn bread
ain't done in
the middle

Happy as
a pig
in mud

# Finding the source of true contentment

We all have our "happiness checklists," don't we? *Once I get this new car . . .* or *Once I buy this house . . .* or *Once I get married . . . then I'll be truly happy.* Do you think that way too? The problem is, when we discover that happiness is just momentary, we keep adding to our lists. But in fact, the Bible tells us that genuine happiness comes from pursuing God's will for us rather than chasing after our own desires. Joy, peace, and contentment can be found only in living for God—not ourselves. Take some time to realign yourself with what God wants. Pray that he will change your heart and mind to discover the source of true happiness.

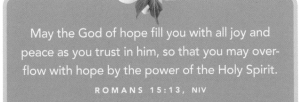

May the God of hope fill you with all joy and peace as you trust in him, so that you may overflow with hope by the power of the Holy Spirit.

**ROMANS 15:13, NIV**

# The sweet power of God's goodness

Uh-oh. You've been working toward some important goals for so long, but you keep running into barriers. Nothing is going well, and life just keeps throwing lemon after lemon at you. Maybe you're ready to give up yet again. But before you surrender to disappointment, remember the question God asked Abraham: "Is anything too hard for the LORD?" (Genesis 18:14). He can absorb the bitterness of life and overcome it with his goodness. Take this hope to heart. Then take a moment with God by pouring yourself some sweet tea and bringing him your lemons.

Don't be afraid, for I am with you. Don't be discouraged, for I am your God. I will strengthen you and help you. I will hold you up with my victorious right hand.

ISAIAH 41:10

The laws of the LORD are true; each one is fair. They are more desirable than gold, even the finest gold. They are sweeter than honey, even honey dripping from the comb.

PSALM 19:9-10

When life gives
you lemons,
put them in your
sweet tea

# Knee-high to a grasshopper

# Embracing the imagination of youth and the wisdom of age

◦━━━━◦━◦━━━━◦

We spend half our lives frustrated that we're too young and the other half moaning that we're too old. But God embraces us at every age. Feeling over the hill lately? As Truvy puts it in *Steel Magnolias*, "Honey, time marches on and eventually you realize it's marchin' across your face." Yet because "wisdom belongs to the aged" (Job 12:12), older people can savor life with more discernment and less drama. Or perhaps you feel too young—knee-high to a grasshopper compared to those you aspire to be like. Yet the Bible speaks of your vision for the future. Paul wrote to Timothy, "Don't let anyone think less of you because you are young" (1 Timothy 4:12). God's ultimate desire is to pour out his Spirit on everyone. And that includes you—no matter your age.

I will pour out my Spirit on all people. Your sons and daughters will prophesy, your old men will dream dreams, your young men will see visions.

JOEL 2:28, NIV

# Turning your anger over to God

Has it gotten the better of you again? An outburst, a fit of rage, a harsh explosion of words? Are you fit to be tied—filled with anger toward someone in particular? You may have every reason to fly off the handle, but anger unchecked reveals a deeper problem. Before you let it go too far, take a break. Breathe deeply and calm down. The Bible says that "people with understanding control their anger" (Proverbs 14:29), so think first about what's going on. Pray for self-control and God's presence in your mind and heart. Let him speak his peace and wisdom to you. Remember, "this world as we know it will soon pass away" (1 Corinthians 7:31). Does that help put things in perspective? Keep your gaze on Jesus, and he will lift you up.

Get rid of all bitterness, rage, anger, harsh words, and slander, as well as all types of evil behavior. Instead, be kind to each other, tenderhearted, forgiving one another, just as God through Christ has forgiven you.

**EPHESIANS 4:31-32**

Pitching a hissy fit

# When life spills all over

You know, there are times in life when things just fall apart.
Even though we try our hardest to play the part of perfection,
there's always drama, and then life becomes a real mess.
Isn't that right? Is that what you're sitting in right now?
Like a glass of milk toppled over, perhaps some kind of mess
has spilled all over you and you're torn up inside by what's
happened. Well, God specializes in messes. Not only can
he turn things around for you; through your mess, he can
also work a miracle *in* you! God "causes everything to work
together for the good" (Romans 8:28), so turn your troubles
over to Jesus. Ask him to make things right. Only he can bless
your mess!

You're blessed when you get your inside world—your mind and
heart—put right. Then you can see God in the outside world.

MATTHEW 5:8, MSG

# Nurturing the gift of kindness

Sometimes we can see it more easily in others than in ourselves: That friend who goes out of her way to brighten the day of someone in need. The acquaintance who unexpectedly says just the right word of encouragement. But is such a gift of kindness present in your own life? Think about this past week—what did you do or say that might have helped others? We often toss around the term *random acts of kindness.* Those deeds are good when they happen, but kindness also needs to be intentional. Right now, think about your day ahead and the people you will encounter. What does each one need? What can you say or do in kindness to enrich each person's life? Stay close to the Lord, and he will grow in you a heart that's pure gold with sprinkles on top.

The Holy Spirit produces this kind of fruit in our lives: love, joy, peace, patience, kindness, goodness, faithfulness, gentleness, and self-control. There is no law against these things!

GALATIANS 5:22-23

*Her heart
is pure gold
with sprinkles
on top*

Stinks
to high
heaven

# Getting rid of the sin in your life

There's a smell in your car. You search the back seat—nothing. You root through the trunk—still nothing. Eventually you look under the front seat, and there it is—leftover lunch from a week ago. Phew! Well, it's not so different in our lives, except we usually know where the sin is hiding. Is that true for you? Do you harbor a secret sin in your life somewhere? Of course, you know God sees it and hates that it's holding you back from his best. The good news is that when we confess our shortcomings to God, leave our old ways behind, and pursue the right path, he'll get rid of the stink. Ask him to forgive you and free you from the stench. Don't hesitate—it's high time for some fresh air!

My wounds fester and stink because of my foolish sins.

**PSALM 38:5**

If we confess our sins to him, he is faithful and just to forgive us our sins and to cleanse us from all wickedness.

**1 JOHN 1:9**

# Praying for the ones who matter most

Usually our anxieties in life circle around the people closest to us—our spouse, children, parents, and friends. Maybe someone has a health crisis, or an adult child is struggling to keep a relationship afloat. Or maybe you're quarreling with a friend. If these kinds of issues are making you toss and turn at night, here's what you can do: Imagine being in the presence of Jesus. He asks, "How's your mama and them?" Of course, he already knows, but he wants you to tell him your worries about each one. As you take each of your loved ones to him in prayer, he is carefully listening. Be assured that he loves them even more than you do. His comforting Spirit will relieve the burdens on your heart and mind.

The prayer of a person living right with God is something powerful to be reckoned with. Elijah, for instance, human just like us, prayed hard that it wouldn't rain, and it didn't—not a drop for three and a half years.

**JAMES 5:16-18, MSG**

How's
your mama
and them?

Your druthers is my ruthers

# Living in alignment with God's will

Sometimes life hands you the blues, and you're not sure why. You feel out of sorts—not just physically, but also emotionally, and maybe spiritually too. Is that where you are today? When life is zigging and you're zagging, it might be that you and God simply aren't in sync. You need some come-to-Jesus time. Find a place to be alone with him and share your feelings of disconnect. Pray about who he wants you to be and what he wants you to focus on. Get yourself in alignment once again with his purposes. Come to the point where you can say, "Your will is what I want, Lord. Your druthers is my ruthers."

Be very careful, then, how you live—not as unwise but as wise, making the most of every opportunity, because the days are evil. Therefore do not be foolish, but understand what the Lord's will is.

EPHESIANS 5:15-17, NIV

# Letting Jesus fix what's crooked

When you're feeling not-so-beautiful, out of sorts, and catercorner with yourself, that's "catawampus." So much can happen in life to leave us that way. If you're in such a spot, consider that so many of the women Jesus encountered were in messy situations. Yet Jesus spoke to them and touched them, making their lives right. Are you any different? Can't Jesus make you right too? Come to him and share how you feel. Let him encourage you and lift you up. Allow him to wrap his arms of love around you. Remember that "the LORD himself goes before you and will be with you; he will never leave you nor forsake you" (Deuteronomy 31:8, NIV). So don't get your feathers ruffled—the good Lord is in the business of fixin' what's crooked.

Every valley shall be filled and every mountain and hill brought low; the crooked places shall be made straight and the rough ways smooth; and all flesh shall see the salvation of God.

LUKE 3:5-6, NKJV

That thing's
all
catawampus

The pot

calling

the kettle

black

# Paying attention to hypocrisy

People today who are turned off by the hypocrisy of religion are simply echoing Jesus' disgust with hypocrites in his own day—in particular, the Pharisees who made up their own rules and expected others to follow them. We rarely notice hypocrisy in ourselves, but is it possible there could be such a problem in your life? Do you condemn others for something, then do the same thing yourself? Be encouraged: If a Pharisee named Paul could repent of his hypocrisy and bring the Good News to millions, then there is also hope for us. With Paul, we can say, "'Christ Jesus came into the world to save sinners'—and I am the worst of them all" (1 Timothy 1:15). And like Paul, we can experience the turnaround of a lifetime.

You who judge others do these very same things. . . . Don't you see how wonderfully kind, tolerant, and patient God is with you? Does this mean nothing to you? Can't you see that his kindness is intended to turn you from your sin?

ROMANS 2:1, 4

# Receiving God's richest blessings

Are you looking for God to bless you in financial or physically tangible ways? He can certainly do that for you, and he probably already has many times before. But earthly blessings are kind of beside the point for God—they are temporary at best. He wants to bless you with far more. Though we're aware that his blessings often come through hardship, it doesn't make our trials any easier. *Why, God?* we wonder. But through hardship, we encounter God's presence and provision. We wind up with the richer blessings from God—the experience of his love and a closer walk with him. As you go through the triumphs and tragedies of life, look for the deeper ways that God blesses your heart.

Even if you suffer for doing what is right, God will reward you for it.

1 PETER 3:14

Though our bodies are dying, our spirits are being renewed every day. For our present troubles are small and won't last very long. Yet they produce for us a glory that vastly outweighs them and will last forever!

2 CORINTHIANS 4:16-17

Bless your heart

It doesn't
amount to a hill
of beans

# Discovering the value of eternal investments

It's no secret that society today has a preoccupation with possessions and money. We're constantly bombarded with the lie that we never have enough. But in the scheme of things, will all our stuff amount to much more than a hill of beans? The Bible makes it clear that money and things will ultimately never satisfy. "You can't take it with you" may be cliché, but it's true. The good news is that God loves us for who we are, not what we own. "If we have enough food and clothing, let us be content" (1 Timothy 6:8). Spend your energy and time investing in pursuits that pay eternal dividends. The rate of return is out of this world!

Don't store up treasures here on earth, where moths eat them and rust destroys them, and where thieves break in and steal. Store your treasures in heaven, where moths and rust cannot destroy, and thieves do not break in and steal. Wherever your treasure is, there the desires of your heart will also be.

**MATTHEW 6:19-21**

# Experiencing God's pleasure
## in the circumstances of life

Maybe it's happened to you: Coincidences. Serendipities. Events that seem random, yet they change your life for the better. When good things occur at just the right time, you might think, *That's funny!* But it isn't chance; it's God's delight working in your life. Have you come to see God as serious and unsmiling? Think again! Our God is a God of joy and laughter. When Sarah overheard the messenger declare that she would bear a son in her old age, she laughed at God's sense of humor. Take comfort in knowing the Lord will "delight in you with gladness. With his love, he will calm all your fears. He will rejoice over you with joyful songs" (Zephaniah 3:17).

Sarah declared, "God has brought me laughter. All who hear about this will laugh with me. Who would have said to Abraham that Sarah would nurse a baby? Yet I have given Abraham a son in his old age!"

**GENESIS 21:6-7**

Funny
as all
get-out

It's so dry
the catfish
are carrying

canteens

# The emptiness of life and the fullness of God

Dry as dust. We get deeply concerned when crops go through periods of drought. Like farmland, we, too, go through times when there's not enough water in our spiritual lives. Maybe you're feeling parched in this season. You've reached a long, arid valley in your journey where there's nothing new—only dust and dirt. Come to your heavenly Father and lay out for him your hunger and thirst. Ask him to transform your wasteland and refresh your world with new life. Jesus says, "Those who drink the water I give will never be thirsty again. It becomes a fresh, bubbling spring within them, giving them eternal life" (John 4:14). He is faithful to quench the thirst of our hearts.

O God, you are my God; I earnestly search for you. My soul thirsts for you; my whole body longs for you in this parched and weary land where there is no water.

**PSALM 63:1**

I am the LORD your God. . . . Open wide your mouth and I will fill it.

**PSALM 81:10, NIV**

# Acting on the practices that bring us closer to God

Sometimes we're fixin' to do something, but we never really quite get around to it. That's true for so many of us. Maybe you've been fixin' to spend more time pursuing God's presence and his truth, but you keep getting distracted. Keep in mind that a Christian is one who acts—not just one who "aims to" accomplish their goals someday. Make a list of all your fixin' tos in your walk with Jesus. Act on one, then another. Soon you'll join the psalmist David in saying, "LORD, I give my life to you" (Psalm 25:1).

What good is it, dear brothers and sisters, if you say you have faith but don't show it by your actions? Can that kind of faith save anyone? . . . You see, faith by itself isn't enough. Unless it produces good deeds, it is dead and useless.

JAMES 2:14, 17

Don't just listen to God's word. You must do what it says. Otherwise, you are only fooling yourselves.

JAMES 1:22

Fixin'
to

She's

as honest as the

day is long

# Becoming the real deal

Most of us have someone in our circles whom we can just plain trust—and like. Everyone agrees that she's as sweet as a Goo Goo Cluster and as authentic as RC Cola. She's honest, consistent, and straightforward in all she says and does. Of course, she's far from perfect, but she'll always be there for you, always be patient with you, and always give you a straight answer—even if it's spiced with a little sass and vinegar. What about you? Are you a person of integrity? If you're open to God's work in your life, he'll shape you into the honest and authentic person he wants you to be. The Holy Spirit always produces the good fruit of honesty. You can become the real deal—a safe harbor for those in need of a genuine friend. Dare to be counter-cultural. Dare to be as honest as the day is long.

The LORD detests lying lips, but he delights
in those who tell the truth.

PROVERBS 12:22

Honesty guides good people; dishonesty
destroys treacherous people.

PROVERBS 11:3

# Riding out the bad weather in your life

Word in the holler says that Dolly Parton made a profound statement: "Storms make trees take deeper roots." Is there a storm heading your way right now? What part of your life is threatened by heavy, dark clouds looming on the horizon? Maybe certain dangers feel as if they might strike close, and you're anxious or fearful. Take a moment to come to God in the quiet before the storm. Remember that he uses the gully washers of life to deepen our faith roots—to strengthen our relationship with him. Don't be afraid to trust him in this bad weather ahead. Think about his great power and love and sovereignty over all things. He is in control.

When Jesus woke up, he rebuked the wind and the raging waves. Suddenly the storm stopped and all was calm. Then he asked them, "Where is your faith?"

LUKE 8:24-25

Peace I leave with you; my peace I give to you. Not as the world gives do I give to you. Let not your hearts be troubled, neither let them be afraid.

JOHN 14:27, ESV

It's
blowin' up
a storm

Stay
classy and
sassy

# Being your best, unique self

We grow up with a lot of people telling us who and what we ought to be. In Fannie Flagg's novel *The All-Girl Filling Station's Last Reunion*, Dr. Shapiro counsels Sookie, "You may not be the person your mother wants you to be, but you are you." Do you hear the voice of your mother, spouse, or someone at work or church echoing inside your head? You would do well to replace it with the voice of God. You see, God created you with a unique personality. Maybe it's big and loud, or maybe it's soft and quiet or something in between. It doesn't matter, because God loves you *for you*. He doesn't want you to conform to someone else's ideal image. Instead, he looks at your heart and embraces who you are deep down. Today, dare to believe that God celebrates when you are comfortable being uniquely you.

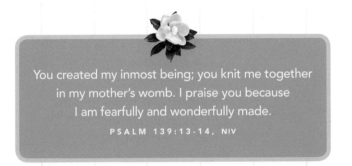

You created my inmost being; you knit me together
in my mother's womb. I praise you because
I am fearfully and wonderfully made.

PSALM 139:13-14, NIV

# When the bad stuff piles up

Has one bad thing after another landed in your path lately?
Are you utterly exasperated and ready to give up? We all go
through times like that, when it seems there's no end in
sight. In these seasons of life, it's important to step on the
brakes—before *you* break. Stop everything and bring your
frustration to God in prayer. Know that he will "personally
go ahead of you" (Deuteronomy 31:8). He'll not only resolve
many of the issues in your life but also give you confidence
and strength to cope. Be patient as you await his answers, and
in the meantime, take every opportunity to cry out to him—
you can even cry out loud if you need to. He'll be there to
wipe away your tears.

The LORD himself will fight for you. Just stay calm.

**EXODUS 14:14**

God's home is now among his people! . . . He will
wipe every tear from their eyes, and there will be
no more death or sorrow or crying or pain.

**REVELATION 21:3-4**

Oh for cryin' out loud!

She's
got
gumption

# Living with courage and grace

How are you living out your faith these days? One of the Bible's extraordinary stories involves Esther, a beautiful young woman who loved God. While the Jewish people were exiled in Persia, the king chose Esther as his queen. At first, she kept her nationality a secret. But when the king decreed the death of all the Jews in Persia, she suddenly faced a crisis. Would she risk her life by appealing to the king and revealing her Jewish identity? With gumption and grace, Esther did so and averted the slaughter of her people. Like Esther, you are called to speak out about your faith and share it with those around you. It may take courage, and it will take grace. Do you have the gumption?

Who knows if perhaps you were made
queen for just such a time as this?

**ESTHER 4:14**

The wicked flee when no one pursues, but
the righteous are bold as a lion.

**PROVERBS 28:1, ESV**

# Finding hope when you don't fit in

Do you feel lonely and isolated—out of place with most everyone around you? Perhaps you're in a new situation, and it's just taking time to connect with others. Or maybe whatever you do or say is at odds with everyone and every-thing. Could it be you have values that aren't shared by others? Although the world says being popular is important, being a follower of Jesus means not conforming to worldly standards. God certainly applauds you for being different, but he also doesn't want you to be lonely. Ask him to provide meaningful friendships, because there ain't a pot too crooked that a lid won't fit—even when those who live out the Bible's truths seem rarer than hen's teeth.

A person standing alone can be attacked and defeated, but two can stand back-to-back and conquer. Three are even better, for a triple-braided cord is not easily broken.

**ECCLESIASTES 4:12**

Walk with the wise and become wise; associate with fools and get in trouble.

**PROVERBS 13:20**

Ain't a pot too crooked that a lid won't fit

# Blessed to be called

_____

# God knows you by name

You may already own one of those T-shirts that says "Blessed to be called" with your name printed underneath. It's a statement that you're proud to be who you are. And you *should* be proud, but maybe for a different reason than you think—not because you've done something to make your name special, but because God made you, redeemed you, and calls you by name. You are blessed because you are a child of God. Right now, take a moment to think about that. Hear God whisper to your heart, *You are mine*. How precious that you are uniquely his—a one-of-a-kind, special, blessed woman. You're not only blessed—you're also a blessing to others. Praise the Lord!

I have redeemed you; I have called you by name, you are mine.

ISAIAH 43:1, ESV

The LORD had said to Abram, . . . "I will make you into a great nation. I will bless you and make you famous, and you will be a blessing to others."

GENESIS 12:1-2

# Saying no to the devil and yes to Jesus

Life is often a struggle, isn't it? On any given day, there are so many ways we are assaulted by setbacks or find ourselves giving in to something we shouldn't do. What vices do you find most difficult to resist? It might be helpful to realize that God's laws against sin aren't just his way of denying you pleasure. In fact, sin is sin because it's bad for you, and God doesn't want you to get hurt. Satan is prowling around, tempting you to do that "one little thing," whispering, *What could go wrong?* He's also busy setting up roadblocks that lead to discouragement. In those moments, do your best to "keep watch and pray," and say to the devil, "Not today, Satan—not today."

[Jesus said,] "Keep watch and pray, so that you will not give in to temptation. For the spirit is willing, but the body is weak!"

**MATTHEW 26:41**

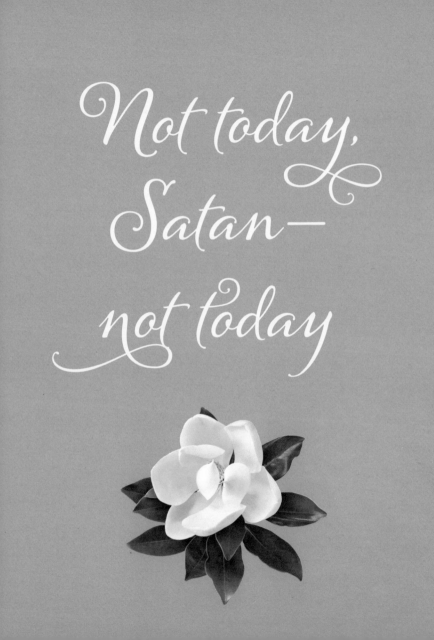

Not today, Satan—
not today

All
chewed up and
spit out

# Dealing with rejection and mistreatment

Everyone, at one time or another, experiences rejection and mistreatment—but knowing that doesn't help when you feel chewed up by life's circumstances. Maybe you've been severely criticized or cast aside—spit out. It's far from pleasant, but know that God holds you close. Jesus, too, was rejected by many of those he came to help. He knows what you're going through. God delights in healing the brokenhearted, including you right now. And he has big plans for your life—in this present world and into eternity. None of what's just happened changes his bigger purposes for you. Bring to God your feelings of rejection. Let him attend to your wounds, and find new strength as you prepare to move on.

He was despised and rejected—a man of sorrows, acquainted with deepest grief. We turned our backs on him and looked the other way. . . . But he was pierced for our rebellion, crushed for our sins. He was beaten so we could be whole. He was whipped so we could be healed.

ISAIAH 53:3, 5

# Waiting for God's timing

Cows *do* come home, of course. Eventually they return to the milking barn, but they take their ever-lovin' time. The Bible tells the story of the Prodigal Son, who demanded his inheritance before his father had even died, then left his family to squander it on a life of sin. You can only imagine his father's heartbreak. One day the son realized he'd blown it and decided to go home. "And while he was still a long way off, his father saw him coming. Filled with love and compassion, he ran to his son, embraced him, and kissed him" (Luke 15:20). Maybe you've been waiting for a long time too. Someone you love has yet to come home. God's timing is often different from ours, but eventually his answer will come. As you wait, continue to lift up faithful prayers to him.

Slowly, steadily, surely, the time approaches when the vision will be fulfilled. If it seems slow, do not despair, for these things will surely come to pass. Just be patient!

HABAKKUK 2:3, TLB

'Til
the cows
come
home

Raised on
sweet tea and
Jesus

# When something else becomes number one

Nothing gets between a girl and her sweet tea, but has something come between you and Jesus? So many activities demand your attention and crowd your schedule. Every to-do item seems important in the moment, but the result is that Jesus is pushed into the back seat of your life. What goal or crisis—or person—has taken a seat in front? When life gets busy, it's easy to neglect the foundation you were raised on. But just because it's easy doesn't make it inevitable. The time has come to put first things first and reembrace the faith principles you learned when you were younger. Pour yourself a glass of sweet tea, sit down at the table, crack open that Bible, and spend time with the Lord. Don't let *anything* come between you and Jesus!

My child, don't forget what I teach you. Always remember what I tell you to do. . . . Remember the LORD in everything you do, and he will show you the right way.

PROVERBS 3:1, 6, GNT

# Surprised by God

When life becomes routine and boring, consider the story of the two disciples who were walking along the road to Emmaus. While they were talking about Jesus' death and the empty tomb, another man joined them and explained how the Scriptures describe how Jesus would suffer, die, and be raised to life again. When they arrived at Emmaus, this mystery man said the blessing before they had supper. Suddenly, the other two recognized that he *was* Jesus! It was their "Heavens to Betsy!" moment. Along your daily walk, don't forget the one who's walking with you. Call out to the Lord; he wants to surprise you with his presence and blessings.

They came to the edge of the village where they were headed. He acted as if he were going on but they pressed him: "Stay and have supper with us." . . . He sat down at the table with them. Taking the bread, he blessed and broke and gave it to them. At that moment, open-eyed, wide-eyed, they recognized him.

LUKE 24:28-31, MSG

Heavens
to Betsy!

No bigger than a minnow in a fishing pond

# God's love overcomes our feelings of insignificance

Has something happened recently that's left you feeling utterly insignificant? Perhaps you were passed over for a promotion at work or omitted from a social invitation. Maybe your life is a sad, lonely song right now and you feel like a minnow in a fishing pond. That's quite understandable, considering the circumstances; but the truth is that your heavenly Father sings a different tune. God created each person to reflect a unique aspect of his infinite personality. Among the myriad of humans on planet Earth, you're one in a billion. He cares about you, celebrates who you are, and loves you deeply and individually. So when you start to feel real small in life, think again about the God who so lovingly made you. The pond might be huge, but you're a rare catch.

You made all the delicate, inner parts of my body. . . .
Your workmanship is marvelous—how well I know it.
You watched me as I was being formed in utter seclusion, as I was woven together in the dark of the womb.

PSALM 139:13-15

# Dealing with impatience

Some mornings it takes forever to wake up the kids and get them dressed, fed, and out of the house. Everyone except you is dragging. Finally you push them through the door, and they're off!—like a herd of turtles. Or perhaps you're frustrated with some of your coworkers or fellow church members: Everyone moves as slow as molasses, and it falls on you to make sure everything gets done. Sure, there are good reasons to feel impatient sometimes, but life is much more enjoyable when you stop trying to control what you can't. The best policy is to let go and let God—pray that his will is done. Leave the herding to the Good Shepherd. Perhaps he might yet transform your tortoises into hares.

You can make many plans, but the LORD's purpose will prevail.

**PROVERBS 19:21**

He will tend his flock like a shepherd; he will gather
the lambs in his arms; he will carry them in his bosom,
and gently lead those that are with young.

**ISAIAH 40:11, ESV**

Off
like a herd of
turtles

Living
in high
cotton

# Praising God for his lavish gifts

Has an unexpected blessing come your way recently—a pay raise or a surprise gift? There are times we come into high cotton, and it helps our lot in life immensely. But have you remembered to thank God for his favor? Maybe in your busyness you've overlooked that. It's funny how we often pray that God will provide, but when he does, we don't even acknowledge it. And we often miss the biblical principle that God blesses us so we can bless others. Will you bring your high cotton before God today and thank him for all he has given you? And don't forget to ask him how you, in turn, can help others. Remember, "God loves a person who gives cheerfully" (2 Corinthians 9:7)!

God is the one who provides seed for the farmer and then bread to eat. In the same way, he will provide and increase your resources and then produce a great harvest of generosity in you.

2 CORINTHIANS 9:10

# How God specializes in transforming hearts

Every New Year's Day, millions make resolutions to develop better habits. It's not a bad thing to do, but the fact is, by the end of the first week, most folks have already abandoned their new goals. Change is hard. Just like you can't make a silk purse out of a sow's ear, you can't perfect your sinful human heart through your own efforts. Lasting transformation *is* possible—but only with God's help. Jesus says, "Apart from me you can do nothing." Those are strong words! *Nothing?* Well, you might accomplish *something*, but it won't last—and what good is that? "I appointed you to go and produce lasting fruit," Jesus emphasizes in John 15:16. There's no shame in admitting to the Lord that you need a boost from him. With your cooperation, he'll refashion your heart—and your habits.

> I am the vine; you are the branches. Those who remain in me, and I in them, will produce much fruit. For apart from me you can do nothing.
>
> **JOHN 15:5**

You can't make
a silk purse
out of a sow's ear

# Remember how much God loves you

Imagine you're putting your child to bed one night. After a story and prayers, you give her a hug and say, "I love you, sweetheart." She asks, "How much do you love me?" And you reply, "I love you a bushel and a peck and a hug around the neck." That means you love her lots and lots. At times you might ask God the same question. On a hard day when you struggle with difficult circumstances, you cry out, "Why me, God? Don't you love me?" And God answers, *I love you so much that I gave my Son, Jesus, so we could be together*. That's much more than a bushel and a peck, don't you think? And it's one long, wonderful, eternal hug around the neck.

This is how much God loved the world: He gave his Son, his one and only Son. And this is why: so that no one need be destroyed; by believing in him, anyone can have a whole and lasting life.

**JOHN 3:16, MSG**

# Resisting the pull of popular culture

You might remember the old song "This World Is Not My Home." The Bible says that as followers of Jesus, we belong to a different Kingdom. The world as we know it is temporary, and heaven awaits us. Yet so often we grab on to the ways of the world like there's no tomorrow. Do you find yourself embracing popular culture more than you embrace Jesus? Remember that as God's child, you really ain't from 'round here—and you ain't supposed to be. You're a royal priest, and "as a result, you can show others the goodness of God, for he called you out of the darkness into his wonderful light" (1 Peter 2:9). Now that's Good News for everyone!

This world is not our permanent home; we are looking forward to a home yet to come.

**HEBREWS 13:14**

Don't copy the behavior and customs of this world, but let God transform you into a new person by changing the way you think.

**ROMANS 12:2**

Y'all ain't from 'round here

I'm just fine,
thank you
very much!

# When you're suffering inside and don't know where to turn

Do you ever feel so empty inside that you don't even know what to say to God? Maybe your pain is coming from a variety of sources, and you can't pinpoint the main cause. You're just plain suffering. When folks ask how you are, it's easiest to simply say "I'm fine." Still, denying the ache doesn't make it go away. What you need instead is a good dose of the Holy Spirit. "The Advocate" (John 14:26) lives inside the hearts of his children to comfort and teach them. Have no doubt that the Holy Spirit wants to help you in your weakness—in this anguish you're feeling. Spend some time with him and release the turmoil. Listen for the whispers that communicate his love. Then it won't be long before you can truthfully say, "I'm just fine, thank you very much!"

The Holy Spirit helps us in our weakness. For example, we don't know what God wants us to pray for. But the Holy Spirit prays for us with groanings that cannot be expressed in words.

ROMANS 8:26

# The benefits of working hard

Which method describes your style—tackling a project and finishing it as quickly as possible or taking your sweet time and enjoying the process? Perhaps there's not a wrong way to approach the work in our lives as long as we're faithful to see that it's done well. But the Bible is certainly clear on a few points: "Those unwilling to work will not get to eat" (2 Thessalonians 3:10) and "This is the only work God wants from you: Believe in the one he has sent" (John 6:29). Work is a gift that brings about our livelihood, and it should be rooted in our faith in Jesus and his desire to bring salvation and healing to a broken world. Can he count on you to help him git 'r done?

Work willingly at whatever you do, as though you were working for the Lord rather than for people.

COLOSSIANS 3:23

Do not work for food that spoils, but for food that endures to eternal life, which the Son of Man will give you.

JOHN 6:27, NIV

Git 'r done

# When you know you've done wrong

Can you remember a time when you were a little girl and did something wrong? You felt so guilty. Maybe you tried to hide it from your parents, and your life was nothing but misery because of it. Now you're all grown, but you're in the same boat. Once again, you feel guilty, and it's burning you up inside. But you can take care of this right now by turning it over to Jesus. Pray, "Lord Jesus, I come to you and admit that I've messed up. Please forgive me. I don't deserve it, Lord, but I know you're merciful. Thank you for making things right." And don't worry—he surely will.

People who conceal their sins will not prosper, but if they
confess and turn from them, they will receive mercy.

PROVERBS 28:13

Let all that I am praise the LORD; may I never forget
the good things he does for me. He forgives all my sins
and heals all my diseases. He redeems me from death
and crowns me with love and tender mercies.

PSALM 103:2-4

# Sharing Jesus with those beyond your comfort zone

As a Christian, how do you share about your faith in God and the new life Jesus has given you? Is your witness only to those in church and to other Christians? Are you preaching to the choir? Think about those you encounter in daily life who might not be in your comfort zone. Is there an opportunity to share your faith with them? To be effective, you don't have to preach *at* them; you can simply let your lifestyle be an example of Jesus *to* them. There's a big world out there filled with folks who've never even heard of the choir. They need to know the Jesus you follow and love. Will you introduce them?

[Jesus] ordered us to preach everywhere and to testify that Jesus is the one appointed by God to be the judge of all—the living and the dead. He is the one all the prophets testified about, saying that everyone who believes in him will have their sins forgiven through his name.

ACTS 10:42-43

# Preaching to the choir

'Prishate it!

# Growing a life of thankfulness

You know you're in the country when someone responds with *'Prishate it!* after you've done something nice for them. Sure, the remark comes off as a common phrase, but often the heart behind it is genuine. It's a lesson for all of us in the kind of life God wants us to lead. The Bible speaks of thankfulness as a virtue, and it's an area of character that God is calling many of us to work on. When we choose to find something to be thankful for, especially in difficult circumstances, we're more apt to have peace in our hearts and a healthy perspective on whatever might be troubling us. Think about the people you might encounter today—at work, at home, at church, at the store—and imagine how you might be able to express your 'prishation when they do something swell for you.

Be thankful in all circumstances, for this is God's
will for you who belong to Christ Jesus.

1 THESSALONIANS 5:18

Let the peace that comes from Christ rule in your
hearts. For as members of one body you are called
to live in peace. And always be thankful.

COLOSSIANS 3:15

# When you're at the end of your rope

Whatever it is, it's knocked you down. Maybe you've tried and tried, only to be broken once again. You're beyond despair, you're exhausted, and you're done. Well, think about this: In your brokenness, God has you right where he wants you. Because just maybe you've been trying to do too much on your own, girl. Perhaps at this point, when you have nothing left, you will finally rely on God. He wants you to come to him in your utter brokenness. Now, finally, he can work with you. Let him give you his strength. Then dust yourself off, fix your ponytail, and with the power of the almighty Lord, get back out there and try again!

You're blessed when you're at the end of your rope. With less of you there is more of God and his rule. You're blessed when you feel you've lost what is most dear to you. Only then can you be embraced by the One most dear to you.

MATTHEW 5:3-4, MSG

Fix your
ponytail
and try again

*Just piddlin' around*

# Get yourself up and get going!

There's always a good reason for making time for rest. And we definitely shouldn't just fill our lives with "busy." But could many of the activities on our calendars be classified as trivial, not really worthwhile? Are some of us really just piddlin' around? If it's time to zero in on God's goals for your life, then ask him for wisdom. "He will give it to you. He will not rebuke you for asking" (James 1:5). We all know our days on earth are numbered. And while we're here, we have the privilege of doing God's work. What talents has he given you to bring to the table? Regardless of how you're gifted, you could always lend a hand to someone in need. Pray for God's direction, priorities, and energy. Rise up with purpose and do great things for God!

LORD, . . . remind me that my days are numbered—how fleeting my life is. You have made my life no longer than the width of my hand. My entire lifetime is just a moment to you.

**PSALM 39:4-5**

# Appreciating the abundance of the Lord

Sure, life can be tough. And no matter what we go through, the joy of the Lord is always there to sustain us. But let's not forget about the good times, when the sun keeps shining and we're full as ticks with one blessing after another! For some, perhaps, this describes the pleasures of a bygone childhood. For others, it might capture the joys of raising their own young 'uns. The point is, there *are* those moments when life *can be* idyllic. "Whatever is good and perfect is a gift coming down to us from God our Father" (James 1:17), who loves us dearly. No shame here in enjoying the abundance of God's blessings! Bask in the joy and delight of being God's kid.

May you experience the love of Christ. . . . Then you will be made complete with all the fullness of life and power that comes from God.

EPHESIANS 3:19

From his abundance we have all received one gracious blessing after another.

JOHN 1:16

As
I live
and
breathe!

# When Jesus calls you by name

The unexpected can hit us in a variety of ways—either good or bad. The Bible tells a story about a woman who had the shock of a lifetime. Mary Magdalene was grief stricken as she went to visit Jesus' tomb. Imagine her surprise when she discovered it was empty! But the drama wasn't over yet. As she started to leave, a man struck up a conversation. She thought she was talking to the gardener—until he called her by name: "Mary!" Suddenly, she recognized him. It was Jesus! Think of her astonishment to see Jesus alive. What about you? Are you amazed at the work Jesus has done in your life? Isn't it incredible that you're on a personal walk with him? Listen for his voice and look for his presence in all you do. Rest assured—as you live and breathe, he is calling you by name.

You make known to me the path of life; you will fill me with joy in your presence, with eternal pleasures at your right hand.

**PSALM 16:11, NIV**

# Saved from the penalty of our sins

Make a list of a few of your favorite things. What are they?
You naturally wrote down several physical possessions,
perhaps including your car, a few gadgets, or your comfy
and welcoming front porch. And, of course, you think of
your family and friends who are special to you. Sometimes a
favorite thing is in a moment—say, on a very hot day, a patch
of shade and a refreshing glass of lemonade. But your list
might overlook the most important item of all: God's grace.
It's the reason we have the assurance of living with God for
eternity. God's grace rescues us from the death penalty for
our sins and gives us so much more. Yes, we can get by on
God's grace. In fact, his grace is the only way we can get by.
The lemonade is optional.

Just as sin ruled over all people and brought them
to death, now God's wonderful grace rules instead,
giving us right standing with God and resulting in
eternal life through Jesus Christ our Lord.

**ROMANS 5:21**

You can
get by on
lemonade and
God's grace

# The joy of living in the Spirit

In spite of the difficult circumstances and uncertainties that life brings, the Good News is that all who love Jesus are for-given and free—children of God who have his Holy Spirit within. After the Lord rescued him from his enemies, King David wrote, "You have turned my mourning into joyful dancing" (Psalm 30:11). Even in the middle of hardships, the party goes on because the Holy Spirit is comforting us and giving us joy. As the saying goes, "There ain't no party like a Holy Ghost party!" Scripture commands us to "always be joyful" and "never stop praying" (1 Thessalonians 5:16-17). Today, let yourself celebrate God's presence in your life. Join the party!

For everything there is a season. . . . A time
to grieve and a time to dance.

**ECCLESIASTES 3:1, 4**

The Spirit himself testifies with our spirit that we are God's
children. Now if we are children, then we are heirs . . . if indeed we
share in his sufferings in order that we may also share in his glory.

**ROMANS 8:16-17, NIV**

# Notes

## THAT DOG WON'T HUNT

*"Don't give up before the miracle happens."* Fannie Flagg, *I Still Dream about You* (New York: Ballantine Books, 2010), 310.

## KNEE-HIGH TO A GRASSHOPPER

*"Honey, time marches on and eventually you realize it's marchin' across your face."* Melissa Locker, "14 Things We Learned about Friendship from Steel Magnolias," *Southern Living*, accessed January 30, 2019, https://www.southernliving.com/culture/steel-magnolias-friendship.

## STAY CLASSY AND SASSY

*"You may not be the person your mother wants you to be, but you are you."* Fannie Flagg, *The All-Girl Filling Station's Last Reunion* (New York: Random House, 2014), 151.